Professionally trained as an actress, MJ Fuller has always been interested in creative writing. Often, she found herself writing poetry as a way of expressing herself, which was always well received by her peers. Eventually, she decided to take the plunge and put together a manuscript of her work. *Sad, Sardonic and Hopeful* is her first contribution to the literary world.

For my mum and dad, who raised the satanic version of myself for 29 years, and then got lucky. And for James, to whom I owe my self-belief.

MJ Fuller

Sad, Sardonic and Hopeful

AUSTIN MACAULEY PUBLISHERS™

LONDON • CAMBRIDGE • NEW YORK • SHARJAH

A CIP catalogue record for this title is available from the British Library.

ISBN 9781398447943 (Paperback)
ISBN 9781398447950 (ePub e-book)

www.austinmacauley.com

First Published 2022
Austin Macauley Publishers Ltd®
1 Canada Square
Canary Wharf
London
E14 5AA

I'd like to thank my family and friends, for putting up with my neuroticism which, in effect, led to these poems.

My parents and husband, for the encouragement that gave me the confidence to get my work out into the public eye; for that I am forever grateful.

I would also like to thank all the staff at Austin Macauley Publishers, without whom this would not have been possible.

After years of being told to write down my sardonic musings, I finally took the plunge. These poems explore the various thoughts that I, and others, have had at various points in life and are easily read and accessible for all.

When I began writing, I noticed that poetry that rhymed appeared to be a bit of an enigma these days, so I have specifically created rhyming poems that take the reader on a journey. That journey can be happy, sad, comedic, tragic, or whimsical, but it's certainly a journey, and I hope you, yes you, enjoy reading them.

About the Poet

I'm the sleepiest girl to walk this Earth,
while you're all out enjoying your mirth.
I sit and ponder what it would be like,
to sit late with drinks or go and hike.
"So why don't you?" you say, and all the while,
I sigh, look down, give a knowing smile:
"Last year, I had brain surgeries – three,
so I'm not like you and you aren't like me.
It's not that I don't want the fullest of lives,
it's because I fear the pain of those stabbing knives
that I know I'll feel if I don't get my sleep,
you'll be out and me? I won't make a peep.
I used to be like you, you see,
but now I'm not like you and you aren't like me."

Be Kind

He hears the footsteps of people
and he shuffles out into view,
they glance at him, then away,
this feeling isn't new.

It's 7 o'clock in the morning.
There's ice on the ground,
but he needs to be here
to get whatever can be found.

It's 7:45 and he shivers,
no one has stopped at all.
He has no choice but to stay here
as he is only moved on at the mall.

8:15 and his fingers are blue
but still his efforts are moot.
He removes his hat to place on the floor
and stares at the holes in his boots.

By 10am he's made two pounds
in only coppers and small change.

He has enough to warm his hands now,
a warm drink he can arrange.

But what of that empty feeling
deep within his gut?
He hasn't had a meal for days…
the shelters are full or shut.

He gets his hot drink and sits
back in his place on the floor.
He once again silently waits
hoping people will give him some more.

People assume he's a vagrant;
someone who you can look past,
but this is all quite new to him
for his potential was very vast.

He'd started a new venture
and things were going very well.
Then corona virus hit the earth
and everything went to hell.

He lost his missus and children
and they took away his home
because his business was interrupted.
So now the streets he roams.

No salvation to him was granted
by the government he voted in.
Now he has no fixed abode
and he's to take it on the chin.

He had great plans for the future
and he had his investors' support.
But his business was damned from the start.
So now he spends frozen nights distraught.

The Song has Lost all Meaning

Pulling off my socks,
another day spent in the house,
I stare outside the window,
all is as quiet as a mouse.
The trees don't even sway
in the vibrant evening sun,
the fluffy clouds rigid,
there are no sounds of evening fun.
Maybe in the distance,
a child screams with delight,
as her father lifts her to the ceiling
before she settles in for the night.
For children, this time is precious,
a time when parents are at home.
For lone adults, this time is tedious,
as we can't even roam.
Police walk our local streets
and ask us what we're buying.
We tell them it's our weekly shop;
six hundred and fifty pounds, if you're lying!
It's for our safety – of course, it is,

but it all feels a little Orwell,
if people stand just a bit too close,
it's like an unexploded bombshell.
Fights break out between upstanding men,
"Your wife just pushed past mine!
She should look where she's going, mate!"
"Yeah? Well, yours should stay behind the line!"
It's true that lines are painted
on every different floor;
signs are outside every shop,
they just wish they could do more,
to protect their staff,
and customers alike.
They are doing what they can
to prevent another virus spike.
Deaths; they rise every day
and cases increase, too.
We're just waiting for that dip,
so that we can do something new.
It's funny that this virus
is so beyond what we know,
that the best advise we're offered,
is how to cough and blow your nose.
We're also told to wash our hands,
while singing birthday greetings.
I have moments of faith that this won't last,
but they are always fleeting.
Tests are offered to the heroes,
and the weak are tested too,
but if a healthy person gets sick,
well…they won't be testing you!

It's all a bit doom and gloom,
this very tragic year.
It went from being so positive,
to us all living in fear.
And why has this happened?
What caused fate to don his hat?
He stepped out to greet us all,
because some tosser ate a bat.

Home Improvement

Walking around the corner,
I hit an on-foot traffic jam.
In the spot right in front of me,
there is an irate man.

We are all at a standstill,
no one's going anywhere,
two people ahead a woman steps out,
and runs her hands through her hair.

She stands on her tiptoes,
she looks straight at me.
I turn to check what is behind…
Lines of people is all I see!

The minutes drag on by,
while we amble slowly forwards.
We pile into a cordoned line,
where there are people in their hoards.

I enter the *exciting* venue,
and quickly look back at the road,

the queue keeps going for miles and miles,
I've never seen such a desperate load!

Inside this place is not much better,
we slowly walk on round.
I always thought this place caused stress,
it's worse with lines on the ground.

Ahead is a commotion,
so everyone stops and stares,
a couple in a heated row,
oh, what a scandalous affair!

HE wants the blue one,
but SHE wants the white.
Even before they get to flat packing,
they've broken out into this fight.

Over by the refrigerator,
a child is screaming, attracts a crowd,
he desperately wants those meatballs,
"No, Timmy! You're not allowed!"

I've got my fan and desk chair,
and I'm ready to go home;
this trauma is now over,
so I give my things to Jerome.

He scans them through and smiles,
"That'll be thirty-five ninety-nine,"
I hand him my credit card…
I can almost taste the finish line!

I look at the queue behind me,
and think I've got out just in time,
"Thank you for shopping at IKEA today,
did you know you can shop online?"

A Letter from a
Drowning Nation

Please, Mr. Prime Minister,
explain something to me:
What good is closing pubs at 10?
The point I just don't see.
It seems a little arbitrary,
or maybe I'm being obtuse,
so forgive me for saying
but I can see why you get abuse!
I know the position is tough
and the lines are very fine,
but I am just beginning to feel
that we are a little bit pushed for time?
The figures are in their thousands
and they are increasing by the day,
so maybe look for other options?
There must be another way!
I know the economy is on its knees
and its people are close behind,
some are even at breaking point
and close to losing their minds,
but maybe just a blanket rule?

A two-week group attempt?
Where everyone must stay inside,
and only REAL key workers are exempt.
Close the borders of the country
just for two little weeks.
Just until the virus dwindles,
and moves beyond its second peak.
Close the offices and pubs,
and maybe the schools too.
Make it an obligatory family staycation,
for all including you!
If the virus spread is caused through contact,
then shut the whole country down…
but only for two weeks,
so the economy doesn't drown.

An Incompetent Announcement

So here we are again, my friends,
the numbers rising by the day.
The government reinstates several rules,
to try and keep the threat at bay.

No more than six outside the house,
no more than this inside, too.
Please remember to wash your hands,
especially when using the loo.

And please remember, teens,
though you may not think you can,
if you break the rules in place,
you'll end up killing gran!

So stay inside – don't socialise…
But go to work all day;
the virus definitely recognises,
the difference between work and play.

It's also known for avoiding uniform,
so please send your kids to school.

They won't be touched while they're there;
don't worry, we have the tools!

But just remember everyone,
it will attack the random social hubs!
However; it's totally safe to meet six of your friends,
if you head on to the pub.

A Break Down
(That Started in 2018)

I've lost where we are here,
the world has gone mad.
There's so much upheaval,
but not all reasons are bad.

First, men were called out,
this made me quite glad,
for taking advantage of women,
who were scantily clad.

Things calmed down for a bit,
after hashtags of 'me-too',
so we all relaxed and settled,
as we thought we had got through.

Until…

Trump got all uppity,
and started a war.
He screwed up trade with China,
tensions grew high and what's more…

Mexico is still on his radar!
He's still hell-bent on removing them all,
as he proclaims to his followers,
"We are still building that wall!"

2019 rolled in without us batting an eye;
2018's problems still there to contend,
but what's more, Great Britannia
with a BREXIT that wouldn't end!

We thought it couldn't get worse.
What else could go wrong?
They voted in Boris?!
Oh! BREXIT will be long…

With 'me-too' and Trump,
and Boris, and BREXIT,
and now half of the country,
campaigning for Megxit…

We really thought that this was the end!
It would all calm down now.
We could go back to our lives.
But 2020 had to worsen it somehow.

At the very start,
it came in with a bang,
with China diseased,
and no emergency plan.

The virus spread the globe,
in a mere few weeks.
Everyone was involved,
even the meek.

Months down the line,
we are trapped in the house.
No one dares go out,
we haven't the nous.

In the evenings, we watch
the world on our screens
and what do we see?
But the stuff of bad dreams.

A good, honest man,
Just put to his grave,
by some nasty police officer,
who just couldn't behave.

Now this and the virus,
ripped through the world,
Black Lives Matter movements,
that have been unfurled.

Riots and protests,
and fear in us all,
the world has gone nuts now.

I just wait
for its fall.

Trumpeting Clown

The trumpet clown, he stands on the stage
and the people are all ears,
some don't really like the clown –
I hear low level jeers.

He talks and gesticulates,
and makes these odd, repetitive sounds.
His smile doesn't meet his eyes,
and his ego won't meet the ground.

His glistening red face stretches,
as he says his *jokes* out loud:
"Let's all inject ourselves!"
He calls out to the crowd.

He has *billions* of followers,
though none appear to be right here;
women and men they scowl at him…
let's give the trumpet clown a cheer.

Gaia

Crack! An emblazoned glow
fills the sky above me.
All around me, everywhere,
rain pours as far as I see.

The world is rebelling now,
for it has seen a weakness in us.
It gave us its everything,
and now it eyes with distrust.

We smoked, and we littered,
we flew, and we drove,
we built up all the cities;
such a tangled mess we wove.

Now Gaia breathes again –
this is her revenge.
First the bats, and now the storms,
but this is not the end…

Foresight

Looking out the window,
the future's what I see,
it's divided and it's fragile,
like it wasn't meant to be.

The planet has a cancer,
and it's called the human race,
and instead of helping out,
scientists look up into space.

There is a growing rebellion,
for those who wish to stay,
but that is getting out of hand,
as it's their own kind that they slay.

The politicians; they don't help them,
no, their weak stances they do sway;
who is really in charge now?
It's impossible to say.

A blind eye is still turned,
when innocents unfairly die.

The world is getting madder,
and I can only watch and cry.

I look to my seniors,
to help me in my woe,
but as I look more closely,
I see that they are the real foe.

With interest in their finances,
"The economy must live!"
But it will live at what cost?
What else is there to give?

Missed Autumn

Brown leaves appear upon the trees,
the bees disappear from sight,
people wrap themselves in warmer clothes,
and the days, they lose their light.

Pubs begin to light their fires,
and people flock to nearby seats,
and on every chalk pub menu,
is a selection of warming, roasted meats.

Apples fall from orchard trees,
while blackberries are in full force,
and people gorge on apple pies,
with not a glimmer of remorse.

For now's the time to stay nice and warm,
to keep the energy levels high.
The animals go into hibernation,
yet we don't and I ponder why?

It's the time to turn the heating on,
and get the old jumpers out,

while hoping for sparklers and fireworks,
with "ooo" and "ahh" type shouts.

And even though this year may differ,
from the season we love and know,
there's no reason to feel too blue,
over the firework no-show.

Halloween may be cancelled,
but that's not a reason to be sad!
You can still dress up as a vampire –
no one will think you're mad!

Make the most of this season,
do what you can to make it fun,
because things will go back to normal,
next year, when humanity has won.

So practice your firework 'ooos' and 'ahhs',
and practice your vampire hiss;
as next year it will be back on plan,
and we will have what we so missed.

An Indescribable Thing

It's looming in the distance
but it's also here with me,
it sits on my chest at night
and it's sometimes all I see.

It holds my hand while I walk
and it plays with my hair.
I hear it whisper in my ear –
it's with me everywhere.

The secrets it tells me are nasty,
they are rumours and unfair.
If I listen for just a little too long
I may end up in its lair.

It keeps the souls of people
trapped up and scared inside,
but others don't know its power
because if they see it, it runs and hides.

Sometimes they say it's like a dog
but dogs are soft and cute.

And the last time I checked
a dog couldn't make me mute.

Others say it's like a shadow.
That's closer, yes, it's true.
But shadows aren't tangible,
they can't grasp a hold on me and you.

False Pretences

It's hard to be outgoing,
when you feel so scared inside.
This feeling of insignificance,
can be so difficult to hide.

It whispers in your thoughts,
around the people that you know,
you really have to force a smile,
and put on a great show.

Pretend you are so confident,
pretend everything is fine.
Will they see your true feelings?
It's just a matter of time.

In yourself you are quite happy,
and you're quite content,
it's other people's perspectives,
that make you self-resent.

You shouldn't let it get to you,
you shouldn't let it in,

but it's these invisible feelings,
that always seem to win.

A Great Showman

My core has been broken
so many stupid times.
Sometimes on a re-occurring basis,
or when everything seemed fine.

But you take it for granted,
and you know how to play;
you pretend you're devoted,
and won't give the game away.

But your head gives you up,
as do your crystal-clear eyes,
as does your perfect mouth,
when it's screaming with its lies.

The fact that you're screaming,
tells me what I already know,
that you panic with your guilt,
and so put on a good show.

A show of huge frustration,
you're totally outraged,

as though screaming right at me,
will get me on the same damn page.

You

My anxious mind craves your warmth,
so I lay my head upon your chest.
I can hear your beating heart,
and my chaotic thoughts are laid to rest.

Am I?

Lopsided, uneven, and basic,
the features that look at me.
A painful truth fills my heart,
that's very plain to see.

I am not like those faces,
and I'll never be like them, too;
so please forgive that I look at my shoes,
hoping I'm enough for you.

Whispers

Sometimes there is a sadness,
that slowly fills me through,
it's insidious and evil,
something that isn't new.

It tells me all the dark things,
it makes me feel dark too.
It makes me think I have enemies;
it can make an enemy of you.

It stinks of paranoia,
it's anxiety for sure,
and other than popping sickening pills,
it seems there is no cure.

It tells me that you hate me,
that you are no good for me.
I'm just thankful for the fleeting moments
when I can clearly see.

Without those I'd be lost,
and I'd be lonely too,

because I'd believe the feeling,
and I can't face it without you.

Balloon

It was a long time ago,
the day you walked into view,
we each had a balloon to give,
and I gave mine to you.
You eyed me with caution,
you just weren't very sure.
This behaviour panicked me,
so your acceptance, I wanted more.
I'd opened up my heart,
and given what I could,
you took my balloon,
and looked after it like you should.
But then you grew bored,
as we grew in different ways;
you forgot the balloon you had,
and you let it go astray.
It floated into the atmosphere,
and right up out of sight,
and there I was with your balloon,
protecting it with all my might…
I didn't know you'd let it go,
I didn't have a clue,

but suddenly I felt a coldness,
when I was too near to you.
So never mind that old balloon,
that's now drifting up in space,
thankfully I have other balloons,
to keep a smile upon my face.
For those balloons I gave out,
are still down upon this earth,
because those who accepted them,
are still certain of my worth.

Helpless

This fatal palpitation,
tearing the insides,
it's less like a storm,
and more like the tides.

A simple question brings the time,
that it hits the shore,
and only after much chatter
does it fade away once more.

The panic swells inside,
as the tide creeps up the beach:
Please don't bring it up!
I think – to it I beseech.

It's not a threat to life,
no, it is almost worse,
with every new stupid thought
my lips I must purse.

Deep Blue

My heart is like the ocean,
it's beautiful and wild.
It has space for everything,
but the sensitivity of a child.

If I give you just a part of it,
will you keep it safe and well?
Because I need to know you'll be there,
when my tide begins to swell.

Grumpelstiltskin

I may be very grumpy,
yes, some would say that's true,
but the world would be so boring,
if we were all happy just like you.

I'm fine being grumpy,
in fact, I'm quite content,
and just because I'm frowning,
doesn't mean I feel contempt.

I just quite like my pessimism,
or being a realist, as I say,
I refuse to see the positives,
in each and every day.

By being oh-so-grumpy,
the world continues to surprise,
when all the lovely things,
begin to open my scowling eyes.

If I was happy all the time,
I wouldn't appreciate what I do,

as I'd take everything for granted,
and probably get bored, too.

Being grumpy, for the most part,
means a melancholy view...
But it makes the special things so much better,
and that, in particular, is you.

Stone Cold

You met me as a fortress,
with walls so high and thick.
But that wouldn't dissuade you,
for it was me that you had picked.

You grabbed your tools and hammer,
And you slowly chipped away,
until you could see me,
I felt like exposed prey.

You approached me with caution,
and held my hand so tight,
once I stopped trying to flee,
you held on with all your might.

You then took all the bricks,
from my fortress made of stone,
and then you started to build,
the place I now call home.

It's safe and impenetrable,
like my fortress used to be,

but the wonderful big difference,
is that you're now here with me.

Time

Life is too short to think and stare,
whittling away our lives with care.

The years have passed so we should act,
before our life is over and that's a fact.

A bus could cripple or kill us on the morrow,
so why waste time with thoughts of sorrow?

Enjoy what you have, when and while you can,
you'll regret it if you find yourself a lonely man.

So make that leap and do it with joy!
Don't waste your time with being coy!

Take the bull by the horns and the scorpion by its tail,
for the worst that can happen is that you might fail;

At least you can say you lived your life,
that's a story more interesting to your kids and wife.

If it were all correct decisions and winning,
in a world that is full of sinning...

you'd be boring, and your life would be, too.
So go out there and explore, fail, and just be you.

Quantum

It took things beyond my knowledge,
things before the dawn of time,
to make all this massive universe,
what is yours and what is mine.

It took chemical reactions,
That no one would ever see.
It took quantum fluctuations,
to make little old you and me.

Mummy's Little Helper

She opens up a bag,
that is filled with lots of stuff.
She hopes that if she uses it,
it will somehow be enough;
to make her feel more human,
and make her feel like she belongs,
she hopes that they'll accept her,
and it makes her feel like she is strong.
She has to take some with her,
in a small, discreet, hidden bag,
so that if she feels it waning,
she can catch it before the sag.
This stuff is so addictive,
so many need it to feel fine,
but we are all okay without it,
and we just need to learn in time.
Our faces are so beautiful,
just as they are, during the night,
but make-up is the norm now,
and some need it to feel right.

From the Ears of Babes

(For Chai and for Greg)

What's that strange feeling?
A rumbling, a sound.
I wriggle myself on the spot,
to try to turn myself around.

Oh, there it was again,
that low humming purr.
Was that this person?
Could it be her?

Oh no, that feels different.
That's lower, I'm sure.
I wiggle around again,
to try to hear some more.

The sounds are together now,
and in unison they hum;
this is all new to me,
these sounds are so fun.

I think it's who carries me…
the noise who's called 'mum',
and it must be the noise 'dad',
that's got to be the other one.

I like these feelings,
the sounds comfort me.
I can't wait to get out,
and then the sounds I will see.

Days Gone By

(For James)

I miss the days gone by
of Piglet's and Tigger's too,
of Rabbit's and of Eeyore's
and of course, Winnie the Pooh.

The days of simple innocence,
where right was right and wrong was wrong,
everything was so exciting,
and the days seemed extra-long.

You would play safari in the garden,
you'd play hide-and-seek in the house,
and when your mother called you in,
you'd hide as silent as a mouse.

Even food was an adventure,
where your peas became the tide,
and your fish finger would fight against them,
until your mouth you opened wide.

And even your mouth was part of it,
of this fun dinner time game;
you became a terrifying sea monster,
seen so often it was famed!

And then came the night times,
where you'd snuggle up in bed;
your parents reading bedtime stories,
so that delight filled your head.

I miss those times gone by,
the golden days of old,
where each day was an adventure
waiting to unfold.

No More

A last boom in the distance,
and everything was done.
The ceasefire had happened,
and the war was finally won.

Silence filled the air,
so the birds could finally sound,
it was so deafeningly quiet,
you could hear a pin drop to the ground.

No more the clatter of bombshells,
no more the gun, sputtering sound,
no more the sound of flying dirt,
the silence was just profound.

No more the cries of soldiers,
screaming in pain into the night.
No more the sound of front liners,
running with all their might.

No more desperation,
no more fear of Jerry,

the soldiers could get on now,
they could finally be merry.

They'd survived the impossible,
they'd made their way through hell,
they could return to Britain,
and have their war stories to tell.

No more the prison of their trenches,
it was safe to freely roam,
no more the fear of when death would come,
they would finally be going home.

Parlez-Vous Anglais?

The English language is confusing,
filled with funny spelled words.
Some are just fantastic,
and others are absurd!
If we take com-for-table for instance:
a very common word,
that's not even how we say it,
no! It's *cumfitable* that's heard.
Unless you live in Yorkshire,
then it's closer, that is true,
but what about those non-native speakers?
It must be so difficult for you!
Then even English-speaking countries,
struggle with their mother tongue;
is it *lie-cester* or *lester*?
Please just help, tell us which one?
Then we have the use of there,
wait, is it their, they're or there?
Honestly, this is getting silly now,
and it really isn't fair!
Then there is another word,
and that's the simple bear,

but do we mean a burden,
or a creature from a den or lair?
Then there are the dying words,
like to be pulchritudinous,
it actually means alluring,
so don't use it to sound studious!
Let's not even mention slang,
that has come into fruition,
to be honest it was hard enough,
without all these additions!

Trick? Or Treat?

Anonymity is the plat du jour,
the children come out to play.
They each wear a frightening mask,
and they come from every way.

The first knock on your door,
you hope it's someone you know,
the shrieks of "trick or treat" are heard,
sweets at them you throw.

All the while you gasp in fear,
to appease their young vibrant minds;
but really, you're hoping you've given enough,
to make sure that they are kind.

The parents eye you with judgement,
as you dish out the sugary snacks.
They are checking that you're being fair,
when you hand out the Haribo packs.

Then all the scary costumes,
make their way back to their home.
This is when the real fear starts…
When anyone the streets does roam.